Christmas
A Joyful Heritage

Compiled and Edited by Susan Arrington Madsen
Illustrated by Glen Edwards

With a Foreword by Leonard J. Arrington

Deseret Book Company
Salt Lake City, Utah

©1984 Deseret Book Company

All rights reserved. No part of this book may be reproduced
in any form or by any means without permission in writing
from the publisher, Deseret Book Company, P.O. Box 30178,
Salt Lake City, Utah 84130.

Deseret Book is a registered trademark of Deseret Book Company.

First printing in paperbound edition, August 1990

Library of Congress Catalog Card Number 84-72519

ISBN 0-87579-367-3

Printed in the United States of America

10   9   8   7   6   5   4   3   2   1

To Dean, with whom every day is Christmas

Contents

Foreword

Alice Ann Paxman wrote that the Christmases of her youth in American Fork, Utah, were "delightful and full of joy." As the snow fell and drifted high against the walls of their tiny cabin, she and her brothers and sisters pulled molasses candy, popped corn, and sang the Christmas carols they knew and loved. Christmas morning there was a single gift for each child: a small doll, homemade cookies or candy, a tin horn, a bag of marbles made of clay, or a new needle and thimble with a spool of thread. After a "sumptuous dinner" and her mother's best plum pudding, father got out his "trick ball" and delighted the children with his juggling.

Similar scenes were repeated hundreds of times during the Christmas seasons of pioneer settlements. Many who experienced these celebrations, modest as they seem today, later claimed that they were the most memorable Christmases they had known: "never to be forgotten, never to be repeated."

We know of such experiences because many, like Alice, kept diaries or wrote their life histories.

Christmases of the middle and late nineteenth century were characteristically family times. Some family gatherings were small, consisting only of the parents and their small children. Others included extended family members who lived close enough to come together. Thomas Cottam, on Christmas day, 1886, counted twenty adults and twenty-four children at his dinner table in the Salt Lake Valley. The Andrew Johnson family of Tooele had a long kitchen table that would seat twenty-four, and it was usually filled twice on Christmas day.

Such gatherings were filled with music, laughter, and the perpetuating of traditions. Amy Brown Lyman, who grew up in Pleasant Grove, Utah, remembered that stockings were not hung up in their home; instead, plates were placed on the table and Santa's gifts were piled on the plates and covered with a tablecloth. When the children came downstairs Christmas morning, "the table looked like a mountain range with high peaks and low valleys." Other traditions, some of which were characteristic of the nations many Saints had emigrated from, included lighted candles in the window sills, the annual Christmas orange in the stocking, and visiting those who were particularly poor with a special gift basket of food.

Family festivities at Christmas time usually culminated in "the meal of the year." Wonderful aromas came from the pioneer stove: roast pork, goose, turkey, mince pies, gingerbread cookies, mounds of potatoes, whole platters of gravy, and a wide variety of home-grown fruits and vegetables. Pioneer mothers boiled everything from beets to squash to make sweetener for candy and jams. "Store-bought candy" was rare and was usually in the diverting shapes of exotic animals. Sarah Bailey Paulsen was delighted to find a piece of wax gum Christmas morning and took special care to make it last for several months.

Not all Christmas meals, of course, were sumptuous. The Alfred Bailey family of Ephraim had a slice of toast Christmas eve. The toast was made by putting the bread on a long English pointed fork that was held over the fire. Afterward, they had a bowl of fried cakes and a glass of milk. Christmas morning, each of the twelve children found in his or her stocking a dozen dried currants wrapped in a little newspaper twisted at the top, along with a lump of sugar.

For the large number of British immigrants, plum pudding was an indispensable part of the Christmas celebration. Ann Mailin Sharp, who lived in Union Fort in the Salt Lake Valley in 1861, described the simple setting for their feast: "Plum pudding, sewed up in a white cloth, was kept boiling for hours in the kettle hanging over the fireplace. The table was set with crude pottery dishes. The food served in these dishes tasted of the clay and was eaten with hand-carved wooden spoons."

Pioneer Christmas treats were homemade, from the candy in the stockings to the suspenders and mittens on the table or under the tree. Elizabeth Parrish wrote that her family saved scraps of colored paper all year to use for Christmas decorations and wrapping paper. Whistles were hand-carved, balls were fashioned from yarn, and dolls were made out of whittled figures, clothespins, or cloth stuffed with sawdust. Isaac Carling, a cabinetmaker, operated a turning lathe and made hundreds of toys for the children of his village. He also made dozens of plaster-of-Paris doll heads, arms, and legs, which the women fitted to cloth bodies. Scores of women worked late evenings for several weeks before Christmas filling the large need for dolls.

In order to ensure survival under precarious conditions, Christmas was sometimes just another day of work. Wilford Woodruff wrote in his diary on Christmas day, 1871, that he had "spent the day husking corn." In 1860 Brigham Young dedicated a schoolroom on Christmas day. Frequently he was in his Salt Lake office for part or all of Christmas day in order to take care of urgent responsibilities.

The Prophet Joseph Smith has several diary entries on

December 25 that make little or no mention at all of it being Christmas. It is clear that for many people, the fall and early winter were occupied with securing the harvest. Many daily journals end abruptly in the fall and begin again in January or February.

Even for those who did chores on Christmas day, most spent the evening in some form of celebration. Many communities sponsored an annual Christmas dance. Pioneer journals include wonderful descriptions of such dances— settlers doing their steps in heavy work boots or, further south, in bare feet. The air was filled with the sounds of a fiddle, accordion, or harmonica. When a group of early settlers gathered for a dance at the home of John Maughan in Wellsville, Utah, in 1859, and found they had no music, Charles Bailey came to their rescue by whistling. He wrote, "In those days I could make as good music as a flute or piccolo."

Lillie G. Barton, in Ephraim in the 1850s, remembered that mothers brought their babies with them to the dance. The baby would be placed safely in a corner of the room, where it would sleep while the parents danced the evening away. When wraps could not be found at the end of the dance, chances were that they had been used by someone to make a "nest" for a baby.

Pioneer settlers also enjoyed going home to home singing with their friends. Hilda Andersson Erickson woke up the day after Christmas in 1881 to the sound of some of her friends serenading her. Henry Clark Jackson, a pioneer of Paradise in Cache Valley, remembered that Christmas Eve always started with a children's choir singing from house to house in the early evening, followed by a group of young teenagers singing from a horse-drawn sleigh, and, finally, at midnight, the fine adult Church choir, which would begin at the bishop's home and then sing carols at other homes in the ward.

John Q. Adams of Centerville wrote that Christmas brought the enjoyment of sleigh riding to many: "The severe winter resulted in the finest open air sport in the world—sleighriding, in big groups, in bob sleighs piled with soft straw, hot bricks and plenty of covers. At Christmas, it is a thrilling new world to participate in, or the sounds at night as you relax in a warm home listening to tinkling bells placed on the harness of the horses drawing merry groups."

Although the real story of early Christmases in the West can be found only in the personal records of those who were there, this collection, *Christmas—A Joyful Heritage*, offers a splendid sample of the hearts and minds of early settlers—what Christmas meant to them in their own words, words written at the time or recorded as remembered in later years.

May this book add to the joy and meaning of your own Christmas season.

Leonard J. Arrington

Preface

Each year since December 1972, my father, Leonard Arrington, has compiled and printed a Christmas card related to Mormon and Western history. With the help of associates, he has gathered excerpts from pioneer journals and diaries describing Christmas experiences. Each year the cards have carried different themes—"Christmas in Pioneer Utah," "Christmas Memories from Scandinavia," "Brigham Young's Christmases."

The response from friends who have received these cards has been so enormously favorable that I felt that others with an interest in the pioneer past would likely enjoy an expanded, book-length collection of such stories.

With the help of Davis Bitton's *Guide to Mormon Diaries and Autobiographies*, I have located several hundred personal accounts of how Christmas was celebrated in the last century. As the reader will see, the experiences of pioneer settlers were as varied as our own.

The accounts I have used are from primary sources housed in the LDS Church Archives in Salt Lake City; the Utah State Historical Society; Special Collections at the Brigham Young University, University of Utah, and Utah State University libraries; and primary material published by the Daughters of Utah Pioneers. Several families have generously given me permission to use items in their private collections. Others who helped me locate material include Jeff Simmonds, Maureen Ursenbach Beecher, Carol Cornwall Madsen, Dean C. Jessee, Ronald W. Walker, and Richard L. Jensen. Helpful suggestions for this project were also made by my brother, Carl Arrington, and Frankie Clark.

I am particularly delighted that Deseret Book Company has agreed to include several illustrations by Professor Glen Edwards, a member of the art department faculty at Utah State University. Glen has achieved national recognition as an illustrator and commercial artist, and his work has enhanced the appearance and value of this collection.

I express sincere appreciation to my father for his help and encouragement with this project. Likewise, I express special gratitude to my husband, Dean Madsen, and my children for their love and support. My husband not only made it possible for me to spend many hours on this project, but he offered valuable editing suggestions as well.

I hope that the personal experiences included in this book will magnify our own joy and pleasure at Christmastime, and, indeed, throughout the year.

Community Celebrations

December 25, 1849

I well remember Brother Brigham's Christmas party of 1849. Like the girls of today, on receiving my invitation the first thought was "nothing to wear." This was literally true, as all our clothing was shabby and patched.

Necessity is the mother of invention, so, after careful consideration, the wagon cover that had done such faithful service during our journey across the plains, was brought out. We couldn't afford canvas and our cover consisted of several thicknesses of unbleached factory cloth. This was carefully dyed and as good luck would have it, it turned out a very pretty brown.

We made this into dresses for myself and sister, trimmed with silk from an old cape of mother's. This cape, black, lined with light brown, not only furnished trimming for our dresses, but I made poke bonnets from the black with quilted lining of the light brown. I had embroidered buckskin mocassins with ravellings from a piece of silk, but I believe for this occasion father, who was a shoemaker, made me a pair of slippers from his old boot legs. I tell you my first ball dress was stunning!

—Susan Wells
Juvenile Instructor, Dec. 1918, p. 631

1890s (Gentile Valley [Thatcher], Idaho)

What a spectacular sight it would be for today's generation to look in upon a remote little group as they gathered for their Christmas celebration. Sleigh loads of people, snug in their quilts spread over a bed of hay, pulling into the Church-yard—men unhitching the teams and tying them to feed—women and children trudging through the snow and up the steps into the small one-room meetinghouse. And inside, the hearty hand-clasping and exchanging of greetings around the roaring hot fire. Men in stiff-front shirts and tight-legged trousers, standing comfortably with their backs to the stove and their hands clasped behind them, teetering on their toes and grinning from ear to ear in admiration of their charming females.

Charming to be sure. On that day of all days, when every female was adorned in a new Christmas frock. Women, stiffly corseted, with their long flowing skirts were grouped about chatting merrily. Maidens with bustles and leg-of-mutton sleeves modestly portrayed their most elegant manners in hopes of attracting the gallant gents. Little girls, quaint in their new togs, strutted like peacocks.

By one o'clock long tables, extending full length of the hall, had been set. Everyone feasted to their heart's content. At two o'clock the old fiddle struck up its favorite, "Turkey In The Straw," and, unable to resist, many of the oldsters chose partners and joined the children in their rollicking hoe-down.

—Lydia Bennett Egbert
Personal History

1907 (La Verkin, Utah)

The La Verkin LDS Ward had their first Christmas party and program in 1907. Bishop Morris Wilson, Jr., hauled a cedar tree in from the foothills. The butt of the tree was thrust into a hub of a wagon wheel which served as a stand. They decorated the tree with threaded popcorn, colorful homemade paper chains and wax candles. They bought mosquito netting from Isom's store in Virgin City and made bags which were filled with nuts and candy as gifts for the children.

The eyes of the children sparkled when the candles were lit and the program was presented. Then old Santa appeared to distribute the sacks of candy and nuts. His cotton beard caught on fire while he was removing the candy from the tree. Mrs. Joseph Gubler began clawing the burning cotton from Old Santa and scratched his face. Although Santa lost his disguise, no serious injury was caused and everyone enjoyed the party.

—Sarah A. Sanders
Treasures of Pioneer History 1 (1952):118

One night when I was sixteen years old, Father gave a Christmas party for his own children and their families and the nearest neighbors. We danced. My brothers were the musicians. We knew it was Father's aim to end the party at ten o'clock, which he did right in the middle of a square-dance by ordering the musicians to stop. But Father didn't know that my brothers had lifted me up to the clock many times that night. Each time I turned it back thirty minutes. It must have been past midnight when the party broke up.

—"Julia's Christmas"
from the Christian Olsen family record
Our Pioneer Heritage 14 (1971):199

December 25, 1880 (Mt. Pleasant, Utah)

Christmas day. We all went to Charley's for dinner and then I went with John Erickson to the dance and danced twenty-five times.

—Hilda Andersson Erickson
Diary

December 25, 1904 (Mendon, Utah)

The Relief Society had a social about this time and five dollars was sent to each missionary out in the field as a Christmas present.

—Isaac Sorensen
Autobiography

December 31, 1879

Coal for the Poor: The Bishops of the various wards are requested to send around to the offices of Abram Gould, Esq., just north of the Deseret Bank, and get each a ton of coal for the poor of their several Wards. It is a Christmas gift from a prominent citizen of Salt Lake, who for years had kept up the annual donation of the charitable present to the poor and needy of our city.

—*Deseret News*

To prepare for the annual Christmas dance, the rough floor of a humble log house was prepared by a process of glazing with wax. Also, a fiddler must be obtained, and he was paid for his services, usually in kind, such as squash, potatoes, cabbage, meat, or the skin of some fur bearing animal. After an opening prayer, the fiddler struck up a signal for the dance to begin. Round and round in different figures the couples marched, followed by the Quadrilles, Polkas, Scotch Reels, and Minuets.

Once in a while a waltz was indulged in, although it was generally discouraged by the General Authorities.

Often a lady was compelled to leave the floor—her baby was crying. No mother remained at home on account of children, except in cases of sickness. Babies were brought along and beds were arranged on seats with coats and shawls for coverings.

—*Monuments to Courage*

Just before Christmas, the Indians would arrive to camp south of town. We were thrilled to see the Indians come, because we knew Christmas was near. The bucks would trail through town, single file, to the store to trade. The squaws and small children would go from house to house begging flour, bread, or dried fruit. The Christmas Eve party was held with the Indians beaming and jabbering over the sacks of candy Santa had given them.

The Oak Creek Brass Band and later the Harmonica Band would serenade from house to house on Christmas and New Year's Day.

—*Echoes of the Sage and Cedars*

Elder Anthony W. Ivins, of the Council of the Twelve Apostles, was known among the Indians in Southern Utah as their friend and benefactor.

On Christmas Eve, Indians had gathered around a crackling bonfire alongside a group of pioneer Saints. Besides the regular Christmas allotment of beef, given to them by the ward, the Indians were to receive something else, no one knew just what. They listened as Brother George Worthen told them in their native tongue of the story of the Christ and his birth. They listened, and then smiled as they recognized the name of their much-loved friend: Anthony Ivins. This year, he had sent them all

Christmas candy, and to old Simon and Shem, the two oldest Indians in Dixie, he had sent warm blankets. The Indians were heard to say as they went happily back to their wigwams, "Tony Ivins, he no cheat. Tony Ivins, he no cheat."

—Washington County DUP Records
Our Pioneer Heritage 14 (1971):204

December 25, 1880

It was here at "Hole in The Rock" that we spent our first Christmas holidays. We children had no place only on the wagon wheels to hang our stockings. Nevertheless old St. Nicholas visited us with parched corn and some cookies which were baked in the dutch ovens. However everybody was happy. We spent most of the day gathering sagebrush to build fires at night to dance by. It was not of course on waxed floors, nor wearing various colored pumps, but it was on the sand rocks and some were barefooted. Brother Charles E. Walton was the orchestra. Sometimes he played the violin and other times the cornet.

—Mary Jane Perkins Wilson
Autobiography

1880s (Franklin County, Idaho)

After the day's celebration, the older children were taken home and tucked snugly in their beds and the parents hurried through their chores and returned to the meetinghouse for their dance, taking their young babies back with them. They put them to bed on benches and made them comfortable with overcoats and blankets. I, being one of the older children, was permitted to watch the babies and see that none of them rolled onto the floor;

and, if any of them cried, I would call their mother. This was my first experience as a "babysitter" and how I loved the job!

—Amanda West Nash
Treasures of Pioneer History 1 (1952):126

December 25, 1860 (Richmond, Utah)

The first Christmas celebrated in Richmond was in 1860 in the new schoolhouse. Every housewife brought an abundance of food. They danced, they sang, and they ate from temporary tables. I remember it all vividly and partly because of an accident. While passing a cup of coffee (made from grains and peas), it was spilled on the head of a child and caused quite an excitement.

—Angus Taylor Wright
Autobiography

December 25, 1877 (Southeastern Nevada)

As the first year of settlement ended in the little town of Bunkerville, twenty-three people made up the community. It had been a struggling year, with no time for fun or recreation in the face of a serious effort for sheer survival. But the crops had been good, so it was decided to celebrate with a dance.

A few rude kerosene lamps gave some illumination, and music was supplied by Ithamar Sprague playing his accordion. Settlers came from near and far and admission was paid in potatoes, pumpkins, squash, or other produce, which was piled near the musician's stand.

Big tables groaned under stacks of refreshments for the dancers, who tromped and stamped with huge work shoes on the rough planking. They loved to dance and this was their first opportunity in more than a year.

They danced with such enthusiasm that every few minutes the floor was cleared so the rough pine splinters could be swept away. Dancing continued until daybreak, when weary couples sorted out their own slumbering children from the heap in back of the musician and made their way to their homes ouf in the sagebrush.

—*An Enduring Legacy* 3:145

(Centerville, Utah)

The severe winter resulted in the finest open air sport in the world—sleighriding, in big groups, in bob sleighs piled with soft straw, hot bricks and plenty of covers. At Christmas, it is a thrilling new world to participate in, or the sounds at night as you relax in a warm home listening to tinkling bells placed on the harness of the horses drawing merry groups. Then there was Christmas skating, in the perfectly flat, smooth lake bottoms west of Centerville, with a big bonfire of cast-off railway ties. And the ice, frozen to a thickness of 18 inches, was soon stored in the co-op store ice house and covered with a thick layer of sawdust and kept for summer use.

—John Q. Adams
Our Pioneer Heritage 18 (1975):158

December 25, 1871 (Kanab, Utah)

It was rainy and the men on the Powell Survey, who were camped just over the Utah-Arizona state line, came to Kanab in the evening to witness a dance that had been announced to take place in the stone building at the corner of the fort. The room was 15 x 30 feet and was lighted by three candles, a kerosene lamp, and a blazing fire of pitch pine.

Two violins were in lively operation, one being played by Lyman Hamblin, the son of Old Jacob, and there was a refreshing air of gaiety about the whole assembly. The dance was opened with a prayer.

Two sets could occupy the floor at one time, and to even things up and prevent anyone from being left out, numbers were given each man, the numbers being called in rotation. None of our party joined in as we were such strangers, but we were made welcome in every respect.

—A Canyon Voyage

December 27, 1873

At 10 o'clock on Christmas morning the children and teachers of the 15th Ward Sunday School in Salt Lake City, numbering about 300, assembled in the schoolhouse, to receive presents which had been placed upon a large Christmas tree in the center of the hall. The tree was illuminated with numerous wax candles, the room having been darkened to give better effect to the scene.

Prizes were distributed. A plain gold ring was awarded to Effie W. Morris, daughter of Elias Morris, for the Best Essay on "the birth and mission of Jesus Christ." There were two other competitors, Misses Maria Olson and Mary A. Jones, whose productions were praiseworthy and creditable. A beautiful album was presented to Thomas F. Howells, Jr., for an essay on the same subject. Prizes were also awarded to the best singers, Miss Annie Jones and Arthur Davis.

—Deseret News

December 25, 1888 (Monticello, Utah)

On Christmas morning, 1888, after a heavy snow the night before, the men cleared the paths with a horse-drawn V-shaped road scraper made from two posts. Then the townspeople assembled at the home of Mrs. S. J. Rogerson for dinner, each bringing food. The table was centered with Mary M. Jones' white frosted cake on a tall glass stand. Mary B. Adams' grape tarts gave the deluxe touch. Children vied with one another in eating bread and butter, mashed potatoes, stewed chicken and gravy, to entitle them to a generous helping of cake and tarts.

Dinner over, the fun began. William Adams danced and sang Irish songs. Emma Hyde, draped in a lace window curtain, stepped to the Highland Fling. Edward Hyde, not to be outdone by his wife, sang "I'm Not As Young As I Used To Be." Then Frederick Jones produced his mouth harp and young and old began to dance.

Hours later, J. E. Rogerson called from the door, "Old Peko is hitched to the cowhide. Anyone want to go home?" With "Good-bye, God Bless You," the party ended.

—The Saga of San Juan

December 25, 1859 (Wellsville, Utah)

We had a dance on Christmas night. . . . Our meetinghouse was very small—14 x 16—and our music was very scarce, only one violin. There were too many for the house, so we divided up and one part went to Brother John Maughan's house. But when we got there we had no music, so I was called to make music for the dance, being a good whistler. John Maughan and Brother Frank Gunnell did the calling. We had a good time all the same. But in those days I could make as good music as a flute or piccolo.

—Charles Ramsden Bailey
Autobiography

(Orderville, Utah)

One December evening some of the sisters of Orderville met to plan a Christmas treat for the children. The Order had no luxuries and the necessities were strictly rationed. About the only sweets the people had was molasses, so, the sisters decided to make molasses candy and cookies for the youngsters.

But on Christmas Eve, they came to "Grandmother Spencer," wife of Howard Orson Spencer, bishop and leader in Orderville, with the news that the brother in charge of the molasses "won't let us have any. He says our allowance for the month is already used." Grandmother's lips tightened. "The children are going to have something for Christmas. I'll speak to my husband after dinner— he'll give us permission."

When her husband came in tired and hungry, Sister Spencer hovered over her husband and after dinner urged him to rest by the fire. As he sat looking drowsily into the flames, she said in a low voice, "You do think the children should have some candy and cookies for Christmas, don't you Howard?" "Ummmhmmm," was the sleepy response, and grandmother went away smiling. She reported to the ladies that everything was all right, "My husband has given us permission." "Did he say we could have the molasses?" asked one doubting Thomas. "He didn't say 'No,'" replied Sister Spencer truthfully. "Now we won't wake up the brother in charge of the molasses. We'll just slip out and take what we need."

The man in charge of the molasses barrel was very conscious of his responsibility. On the lid of the barrel he had placed a section of heavy logging chain and a large boulder. Only a thin wooden partition at the head of the bed separated him from the barrel outside, and he was a light sleeper. Shivering from the cold the women crunched through the snow toward the barrel. It was beginning to snow again and the night was very dark.

With infinite caution they removed the heavy chain without so much as one betraying clank. It took the combined efforts of all the women to lower the boulder noiselessly to the ground. There was a breathless pause as Sister Spencer raised the lid and dipped into the barrel

with a saucepan. She emptied its contents into a bucket
and dipped again, and again. "We have enough now,"
whispered one of the women. "Let's go back." With the
same caution the chain and boulder were replaced and
the women filed back to the warm kitchen to make the
Christmas goodies. But, there was a dismayed gasp when
they looked into the pail. "Oh dear, we haven't enough
molasses. We'll have to get some more." "Oh no, Sister
Spencer. It's cold and dark. It's too risky." "Well, just the
same, we must unless we want the children to be disappointed."

There could only be one answer to such a statement
and the little band of mothers went again to the molasses
barrel. They returned safely and set to work. When morning came, every child in Orderville had two molasses
cookies and one big slightly sticky lump of candy in his
stocking. Santa Claus had not forgotten them. Grandfather insisted all his life that he could not remember ever
having given the women permission to get the molasses.

—*Our Pioneer Heritage* 18 (1975):160-61

It was traditional in Kane County, Utah, for a band to
serenade the citizens on Christmas Eve. The band members were often invited into the homes for refreshments.

The story is told that one time they went into a home
where they were served a dried-peach pie. The filling
lacked sufficient sugar and the crust was a little tough.
When no one was looking, several members of the band
slipped the remainder of their pie into the big bass horn.
Nels Johnson did not see them do this, so when they were
about to leave, he said, "Let's play one more tune for these
good people." "No, it is too late," one of them said. He
persisted, but when he blew into the horn, no sound came

out. Puzzled, he turned the horn upside down and out poured the pieces of pie. The band never again received an invitation to partake of refreshments at that home.

—*History of Kane County*

(Millard County, Utah)

After a Christmas eve program presented by the Primary of the Oak City Ward, an expectant hush fell over the assembled group. Soon Santa's bells could be heard out in the street; the doors were thrown open and in Santa bounced, his cap tassel flapping and his fat tummy shaking as he pushed his wheelbarrow, loaded with peanuts and candy, into the center of the floor. The small children clung to their parents, half in fear and half in wonder, of what was happening. The older children could hardly wait, for soon he began throwing peanuts into the crowd and the scramble began to see who could gather the largest amount. Everyone in town attended this program and the admission was five cents per person. Each person received a bag of candy and nuts prepared by Santa's helpers.

—*Our Pioneer Heritage* 18 (1975):161

Christmas with Early Prophets

Joseph Smith

December 25, 1835 (Kirtland, Ohio)

At home all this day and enjoyed myself with my family, it being Christmas day—the only time I have had this privilege so satisfactorily for a long time.

—Diary

December 26, 1842 (Nauvoo, Illinois)

[Emma] was delivered of a son, which did not survive its birth.

—*History of the Church* 5:209

December 25, 1843 (Joseph Smith's last Christmas; he and Emma were residing in the newly completed Mansion House in Nauvoo, Illinois)

This morning, about one o'clock, I was aroused by an English sister, Lettice Rushton, widow of Richard Rushton, Sen., (who, ten years ago, lost her sight) accompanied by three of her sons, with their wives, and her two daughters, with their husbands, and several of her neighbors, singing, 'Mortals, awake! with angels join' &c., which caused a thrill of pleasure to run through my soul. All of my family and boarders arose to hear the serenade, and I felt to thank my Heavenly Father for their visit, and blessed them in the name of the Lord.

[Later that evening, a large gathering of family and friends "supped" with the Prophet and spent the evening enjoying good music and dancing "in a most cheerful and friendly manner." Then, an uninvited guest interrrupted the party.]

During the festivities, a man with his hair long and falling over his shoulders, and apparently drunk, came in and acted like a Missourian. I requested the captain of the police to put him out of doors. A scuffle ensued, and I had the opportunity to look him full in the face, when to my great surprise and joy untold, I discovered it was my long-tried, warm, but cruelly persecuted friend, Orrin Porter Rockwell, just arrived from nearly a year's imprisonment without conviction, in Missouri.

—History of the Church 6:134-35

Brigham Young

December 25, 1850

Christmas day lovely. The band, twenty-six in number, have promenaded the city and played before the houses of the Presidency, Twelve, and others, while riding on horse-back. President Young went up to his mill, where there was a dance in the upper room.

—Historian's Office Journal

December 25, 1857 (Salt Lake Valley)

Last evening President Young attended a party at the Social Hall. Today he and his brothers and their families met at his house, for a great family meeting where the president talked about his experiences leading the Kingdom, his hopes for the family and the Church, and about doctrine.

—Historian's Office Journal

December 24, 1862 (Salt Lake Valley)

Brigham Young gave a party in the now-completed Salt Lake Theater. The guests were mainly those who had attended the formal dedication of the theater on March 8, 1862. Every seat was taken. Brigham Young greeted his guests, prayers, talks and readings followed. The theater orchestra played "Calanthe Schottische" and the tabernacle Choir sang "On the Mountain Tops Appearing."

President Young then surprised the group by signaling the orchestra members. They started to play "Sir Roger de Coverly." President Young and a selected group danced this popular English dance. The remainder of the time was spent dancing, and all had an opportunity to enjoy themselves. That night the theater opened to the public. Many spent their Christmases at the theater.

—"Yule Celebration Richer with Echo From Pioneers,"
Deseret News, Dec. 14, 1982

Christmas with Brigham Young's family, as remembered by his daughter Clarissa Young Spencer

We hung our stockings on the mantel, for we had no Christmas tree in early days. Christmas bundles came from John Haslam's store, where father had arranged for each individual family's gifts. There were toys, such as bugles or drums for the boys, and beautiful painted rag dolls, that were made by Elsie Long in her little "art" shop near Dinwoodey's store, for the girls. These dolls were not dressed, so we learned to sew for them. Our newest supplies in winter clothing were usually given to us as Christmas gifts. Among them were pretty knitted garters and stockings, mittens and wrist bands. We did not exchange presents. Later, when we had Christmas trees, they were decorated with gold and silver paper ornaments and popcorn. Father did not approve of candles because they were a fire hazard. We had honey taffy, molasses candy and a huge jar of cookies.

—Brigham Young at Home

Wilford Woodruff

December 25, 1836 (Kirtland, Ohio)

Sunday, went up to the house of God to worship and heard a discourse from Brother Samuel Smith. Brother Hyrum Smith broke bread which closed the meeting. Elder Smoot was quite sick and healed by the laying on of hands.

—Diary

December 24, 1850 (Salt Lake Valley)

I spent the time drawing rock from the canyons.

—Diary

December 25-28, 1850

Was spent, most of the time, at hard labor.

—Diary

December 25, 1871

. . . was Christmas, but I spent the day husking corn.

—Diary

December 25, 1874

Christmas. We shot nine ducks.

—Diary

January 6, 1877

You ask what I was doing on Christmas. I spent the whole day at the Temple in St. George. Forty women were sewing carpets and all the men were at work. Josiah Hardy worked at the buzz saw until 9 o'clock at night to get through. We laid carpets, put curtains on the partitions and covered the altars, preparing the temple for its dedication.

—Letter to his wife Emma Smith Woodruff

December 25, 1886

Christmas morning, warm and pleasant. Emma [his wife] had knit 13 pair of mittens in which she put money & candy for the children. Grand Pa and Grand Ma got $2.50 each in their stocking with other things. There is a great time in the street this morning. A band of musicians are serenading before the house and a regular Christmas Holladay. We had our dinner at 3 o'clock. There was 20 grown persons and 24 children at the table. The evening was spent in music and singing.

—Diary

December 25, 1888 (Salt Lake City)

All is astir this morning. The children are examining their presents. Brother Wilkin went out to the penitentiary to take fifty turkeys and get up a Christmas dinner for the prisoners.

—Diary

December 25, 1885 (Salt Lake City)

Christmas Day. I spent the day in the Chamber locked up as a prisoner while all the family went to the ward school house to attend the Christmas (Social). I feel thankful to God I was still a free man on earth.

—Diary

Joseph F. Smith

One day just before Christmas, I left the old home with feelings I cannot describe.

. . . I wanted something to please my chicks and to mark the Christmas day from all other days—but not a cent to do it with! I walked up and down Main Street, looking into the shop windows—into Amussen's jewelry store, into every store—everywhere—and then slunk out of sight of humanity and sat down and wept like a child, until my poured-out grief relieved my aching heart; and after a while returned home, as empty as when I left, and played with the children, grateful and happy only for them.

—*Improvement Era,* Jan. 1919, p. 266

From 1846 to 1849, I knew no Christmas, and no holiday; and, indeed, if we had a Christmas or a New Year celebration at all before 1846—or until after I was married, for the life of me, at this moment, I cannot remember it.

—Letter to his son, December 29, 1914

Heber J. Grant

December 25, 1888 (Salt Lake City)

Spent nearly the entire day at home, took the little ones out in a buggy to make some Christmas presents. I feel truly and sincerely thankful on this Christmas day for all the many blessings me and mine are in enjoyment of.

—Diary

December 25, 1927

Day spent with books. Books! Books! Had lunch at home today for the first time in several days. I am sending books to all the members of the Sunday School Union Board, Y.W. and Y.M.M.I.A., Primary and Relief Society Boards, and to the directors of Z.C.M.I., Home Fire, Beneficial Life Ins. Co., Zions Savings Bank, Union Pacific Railroad Co., (and many others), to say nothing about personal friends. I am sorry to say that all the books have not yet arrived from the Deseret News Press and that part of the books will not reach my friends until after Christmas. I am also . . . giving over one hundred copies of the Lecture on Martin Luther to the employees in the Church offices. Owen and Rachel Heninger have been helping Brother Joseph Anderson and Bertha in mailing these books. I was busy all day principally with books, and have autographed a little over 600 books personally and over 2300 for missionaries. Although my heart, alas, is bigger than my pocketbook, I pray it will stay that way.

—Diary

December 25, 1936

We drove down early in the morning to American Fork and visited with Edith and her family. . . . We returned in time for a family gathering at our house at eleven o'clock. We have forty-seven living grandchildren, ten great-grandchildren, and twelve grandsons-in-law and ten

sons-in-law, which makes quite a tribe when we are together. One of the great-grandchildren, John Taylor Anderson, five years old, put his fingers in his ears and said,
"chatter, chatter, chatter," which accurately describes
what went on.

—Letter to Mr. and Mrs. Theadore Nystrom

George Albert Smith

Christmas Eve, we hung our stockings in front of the
fireplace in the dining room. Father always hung a huge
stocking because he assured us that Santa Claus would
never get all the things he wanted in just a regular stocking. That added to the gaiety of the occasion. Each year
he brought his tall rubber boots from the basement, and
stood one at each side of the fireplace. No matter how
excited we children were, we were never permitted to
go downstairs until we were washed, combed and fully
dressed, then we had morning prayers and sat down to
breakfast—the worst breakfast of the year, because it
took so much time and seemed to hinder our getting to
our stockings.

There was always something very unusual and very
special down in the toe of the stocking. First we laughed
and laughed over the things that Santa Claus put in
father's boots—coal, kindlings, and vegetables. Then we
were offended because we thought Santa Claus was not
very kind to father who was always so generous with everyone else. We always brought something very special the
next day to make up for the slight Santa Claus had made.

After our mirth and merriment had subsided, father
took us with him to make the rounds of the forgotten
friends that he habitually visited on Christmas. Once we
went down a long long alley in the middle of a city block
where there were some very poor houses. We opened the
door of one tiny home and there on the bed lay an old lady

very sad and alone. As we came in, tears ran down her cheeks. She reached over to take hold of father's hands and said, "I am grateful to you for coming, because if you hadn't come, I would have had no Christmas at all. No one else has remembered me." We thoroughly enjoyed this part of the day.

—Emily Smith Stewart, daughter of George Albert Smith

December 25, 1940

It was a real treat to see how happy the children were with their gifts. . . . I played with them, helped them enjoy their toys, read to them some faith-promoting stories and we shed tears together as we had brought to our attention the sacrifices that were made by some of our loved ones when they settled this country.

—Diary

My grandfather, George Albert Smith, had heard my brother, sister and me talk about what we wanted for Christmas for weeks. We described, in detail, what we would get, what color, what size, and on and on.

Christmas Eve finally arrived and we all hung up our stockings on the fireplace mantel, still hoping aloud for LOTS of gifts.

Just before we went to bed, Grandfather said, "Wait a minute, I have to get my stocking." Pretty soon he came back with his blue eyes twinkling. He carried a great big scout sock in his hand. What's more, he had taken a pair of scissors and cut off the toe of the stocking. He hung up his stocking with great glee and then went over and got the empty coal bucket and put it right beneath the stocking.

Well, I was very impressed with how smart Grandfather was. Not only would Santa have to fill his stocking, but he'd have to fill the coal bucket too. What a smart idea!

Christmas morning, after breakfast, we opened the doors to the living room and raced in to where the tree was. I was especially anxious to see what Santa had left Grandfather.

But when I saw his stocking, my heart sank, and my eyes filled with tears, because Santa had left my very SPECIAL Grandfather a switch and coal and onions.

Grandfather saw the tears in my eyes and he pulled me towards him and said, "Now Shauna, you must remember that this is Christ's birthday we are celebrating and even Santa doesn't like to see anyone be greedy."

I learned a great lesson, one I've never forgotten, and one I've always been grateful for.

—Shauna Stewart Larsen, granddaughter of George Albert Smith

First Ten Years
in the Great Basin

1847

December 25 (Salt Lake Valley)

The Christmas of 1847 was fortunately a mild one. There was intense suffering, especially among the women and children. Food was scarce with little variety; there were, of course, no Christmas gifts, and no Christmas trees, but there was a Christmas spirit in the camp.

—"First Christmas in Utah,"
Deseret News, Dec. 7, 1933

December 25

We had no floor but the ground, but we were thankful for a roof. My father laid the floor on Christmas day, and my mother called it a merry Christmas. It was indeed a time of rejoicing; we had been so long without a home and suffered so much living in a wagon during the cold weather."

—Mary Jane Mount Tanner
*A Fragment: The Autobiography
of Mary Jane Mount Tanner*, p. 50

December 25

From the 19th to the 25th of December we had frosty nights and warm days in the valley. The snow is now nearly gone and weather fine. Today (25th) we were awakened by the firing of cannon and the day was spent in work by some, and in amusements by others, and at night dances and plays by the young people.

—Robert Stanton Bliss
Journal

December 25 and 26

I remember our first Christmas in the Valley. We all worked as usual. The men gathered sagebrush, and some plowed; for though it had snowed, the ground was still soft, and the plows were used nearly the entire day. We celebrated the day on the Sabbath (Christmas was on Saturday), when all gathered around the flagpole in the center of the Fort, and there we held a meeting. And what a meeting it was. We sang praises to God, we all joined in the evening prayer, and the speaking that day has always been remembered. There were words of thanksgiving and cheer. Not a despairing word was uttered. The people were hopeful and buoyant because of their faith in the great work they were undertaking. After the meeting there was handshaking all around. Some wept with joy. The children played in the inclosure, and around a sagebrush fire that night. We gathered and sang "Come, Come Ye Saints."

We had boiled rabbit and a little bread for our dinner. Many who were there for that first Christmas in the Valley later remarked that in the sense of perfect peace and good will, they never had a happier Christmas in all their lives.

—Elizabeth Huffaker
Our Pioneer Heritage 14 (1971):204

1848

December 25

The Christmas of 1848 found the pioneers with a much greater variety of things for their dinner. Some had wild duck or prairie chicken and a little cake. Although sugar was scarce, some molasses had been made by squeezing corn stalks, making what they called corn stock molasses. Serviceberries and chokecherries had been gathered from the canyon. Pies were made of these and some gingerbread was mixed and made into various shapes to please the children. They were indeed happy with their cakes. They did not even think of looking for other presents.

—Bryant S. Hinckley
"Christmas With the Pioneers,"
Bryant S. Hinckley papers, Church Archives

December 25

Christmas day, of 1848, was mild, yet the day was dull. It was properly observed in the Infant Colony. The brethren commenced shooting ravens. President Young and Lorenzo B. Young spent the forenoon in the office.

—Historian's Office Journal

December 25

Heber C. Kimball gave a dinner to a few of the brethren and sisters, and Brigham Young with some of his family, and Willard Richards and others of the Apostles were present. The conversation was cheerful, and as Sister Vilate Kimball was the hostess (and was a prime favorite with all the guests), it must have been a very pleasant affair; as for myself, I was too much occupied with my baby to take much notice of the amusements, except that I know Hans played the violin, and Brother Smithies the big bass, and Horace K. Whitney the flute, and of course there was singing—Horace and some of the rest of us used to sing, "Shades of evening close not o'er us," and "Bonnie Doon," and "Maid of Athens." But I don't believe we had presents for the children; I don't know what we could have given them, they were not days of plenty, and we have scarcely become accustomed to our new surroundings. No doubt Heber C. Kimball told some of his funny anecdotes, for he never failed to make merry in that way on all festive occasions.

—Adapted from Emmeline B. Wells
Young Women's Journal 12 (1901):539-42

1849

December 24

Christmas eve was all alive by the people in all directions firing guns, pistols, revolvers, and the cannon fired several times. A dance at Martin H. Peck's, and the band played at Aaron Farr's house.

—Thomas Bullock
Journal

December 25

Tuesday, December 25, 1849, one hundred and fifty persons assembled by invitation at President Young's house in greater Salt Lake City to celebrate Christmas day. The tables were twice filled by the company and all were feasted with the good things of the valley. When the tables were removed, dancing commenced, which was continued with energy, without interruption, except for supper, until a late hour.

—Adapted from "Yule Celebration Richer with Echo from Pioneers"
Deseret News, December 14, 1982

December 25 (Tooele, Utah)

When the children awoke on Christmas morning in 1849, not a doll was to be found in all the land, no, not even a stick of candy, or an apple was found in the cabins. But the children and their parents were happy that they still had a little to eat, and prospects for them in their new homes were beginning to grow brighter each day. Before the day was over, they all had a jolly time.

In the evening they had an old fashioned dance at the cabin of John Rowberry. The only drawback was the music. Not an instrument of any kind was to be found. Cyrus Call was a very good whistler and he whistled tunes while the merry pioneers danced.

—Sarah Lucretia Holbrook Tolman
Treasures of Pioneer Heritage 4 (1955):197-98

1850

December 25 (Salt Lake Valley)

Christmas was a jolly time, though all the fare was simple and the stockings hung in the chimney corner were filled with homemade gifts. The stockings were filled with beet molasses candy made in all kinds of fanciful shapes, and pulled until quite light and brittle, and gingerbread cut into fantastic figures, as well as doughnuts cut and fried beautifully brown; and the girls received rag dolls which they enjoyed singing to sleep with the old-fashioned lullabies. Great care was taken to dress them nicely from the odd bits of various material.

—Adapted from Emmeline B. Wells
Young Women's Journal 12 (1901):539-42

December 28

As many a merry Christmas to our patrons and friends as they are willing to tarry here in mortality to enjoy.

—*Deseret News*

December 25

This is a fine clear cold day. Some snow on the ground but very pleasant under foot. The roads being bare &° smoothe.

The people are taking their Christmas very pleasantly with the exception that Ree's store was broken into last night and robbed. Mostly of wine as I learn. I was around town today enjoying the times by looking on.

—Hosea Stout
Diary

1851

December 25 (Salt Lake Valley)

Wife and I went to a dinner &° quilting at Allen Stout's. I then went up in town to see the operations of Christmas which was carried very largely by the boys serenading in the streets to the great annoyance of the police whose duty it was to keep the peace.

Hosea Stout
—Diary

December 25

A delightful day, ushered in not by the ringing of bells, for our city does not possess any, but by the firing of cannons. At daybreak the Nauvoo Brass Band has assembled and serenaded the city for 2 hours. At 10 a.m. the carpenter's shop was thrown open for an entertainment for the men employed on the public works, who with their families numbered 600 to 700. The building was comfortably fitted up with seats, tables, and conveniences for making tea. The Governor with several members of the Legislature were present with their ladies. When the floor was cleared for dancing (a good band having been engaged) the employers took for their partners the wives and daughters of the workmen and the workmen in turn took the wives and daughters of their employers. The company separated at 10 p.m.

—Jean Rio Baker Pearce
Journal

December 25

Early Christmas morning, several companies of serenaders with brass instruments made the sleeping mountains echo with sounds of rejoicing. Our attention was drawn more particularly to the Governor's Mansion in front of which was drawn up in military order a troop of horseman: there was the Brass Band, giving His Excellency a good wish in sweet strains.

At ten o'clock the Committee of Management was in respectful waiting to receive those who were invited to the Christmas party in the Carpenter's Hall. Now the merry workmen and their happy wives and smiling daughters, clad in genteel apparel, came pouring in from every quarter, loaded with an abundance of luxuries of every description. After a prayer of Thanksgiving was offered, the band struck up a merry tune. We counted from 96 to 144 persons on the floor dancing at once. Each family partook of refreshments and cool clear water from the mountains. The atmosphere was not polluted with tobacco fumes or the drunkard's breath. We thought of the gloomy past and of the glorious present, of the prospective future. We

thought of our friends in other lands wishing they were here with us. Gov. Young spoke, talking on tithing and resolved to build a house unto the Lord where He can come or send His servants. The deep-toned voices of the Public Hands answered "yea." A vote of thanks was given Captain Hooper for his handsome present of candies and raisins to the party and it was given to the poor who could not buy these luxuries.

—G. D. Watts
Deseret News

1852

December 25

When the Social Hall was completed, in 1852, Christmas was celebrated there with dancing parties, both for the adults and the children. Our girls and boys will never forget the first Christmas tree there where there was a present for every child of several large families, and all numbered and arranged in perfect order of name and age. President Young—Brother Brigham—was foremost in making the affair a grand success. Hon. John W. Young, then only a boy, handed the presents down from the tree, and I recollect Brother Brigham standing and pointing with his cane, and telling John just which to take down, and so on; the children were wild with delight and some of the mothers quite as much elated, though not as demonstrative. After the Santa Claus tree was stripped of its gifts, the floor was cleared and the dancing commenced, and there was good music too, and President Young led the dance, and "cut a pigeon wing," to the great delight of the little folks. In fact, I think the evening was almost entirely given up to the children's festivities, and the older ones, the fathers and mothers and more especially President Young, made them supremely happy for that one Christmas eve.

—Adapted from Emmeline B. Wells
Young Women's Journal 12 (1901):539-42

December 25

This Christmas celebration took the form of a dedication. The 14th Ward School House—west on First South—
being finished. The Quorum of the Twelve were repre-
sented by John Taylor, Wilford Woodruff, A. Lyman and
F.D. Richards. Capt. Ballo's band played lively tunes. All
the above Apostles made speeches. They wanted to see
schools established where higher education could be
taught—where the fine men and women of the future
could be trained to carry on the work. Meeting adjourned
at three o'clock when dancing commenced. All were invited. Tickets to the dance cost 50 cents. At twelve o'clock
they closed with prayer.

—Walter Thomson, clerk of the 14th Ward
in Salt Lake City

December 25 (San Bernardino, California)

Weather pleasant though a little cloudy. Night rainy.
The day passed away without any bustle or noise of any
kind, and no one would have known it to be Christmas if
it had not been for the children going about asking for
Christmas gifts.

—San Bernardino Historical Records

1853

*December 25 (Brigham Young addressed a congregation in
the Old Tabernacle. His remarks included these words:)*

Be cautious. Keep your consciences clear & be humble.
Sanctify yourselves. Distress & poverty has never been felt
in this Valley. You will not find a man or woman com-

plain who was here in 1847 or 1848. Take the men &
women who took their lessons with Joseph; they do not
complain. I wish you a Merry Christmas & 10,000 of
them.

—Historian's Office Journal

1854

December 26

The judges of the Supreme Court, Governor Young,
the Presidency of the Church, the Twelve, Col. Steptoe
& officers together with a large number of citizens & resi-
dent strangers were present forming a large assembly.
Every attention was given for our comfort and entertainment. The ballroom was tastily ornamented with cedar
boughs interspersed with wreaths of artificial flowers.
The only objection existing was that the room was too
small for the company although a spacious ballroom. The
company, composed of both saints and sinners, enjoyed
themselves extremely well. Judge Kinney, though a stiff
Presbyterian who never had, as he said, graced a Ballroom
in his life, could not refrain from dancing with a spirit.

About midnight we took supper, an excellent one too,
and returned to the dance, continuing till about three in
the morning when all returned home well satisfied.

—Historian's Office Journal

December 25

I met with the inhabitants of the 14th Ward & delivered an address to the people & was followed by remarks
from Bishop Isaac Morley, Bishop Hoagland & others. We
were dismissed and people spent the afternoon & evening
in the dance. There was a great excitement through our

city during the fore part of the day. Some of the soldiers that were quartered in the heart of our city became intoxicated & began to fight among themselves & soon some of the citizens became mixed with them and the soldiers fired upon the people & the people flung stones in return. Some were wounded on both sides but none killed. The Military officers drove the soldiers into the barracks & the Mayor & Marshall of the city cleared the streets of the citizens which ended the fray.

—Wilford Woodruff
Diary

1855

December 26

Yesterday was "Merry Christmas" which passed with unusual quietness. Although many went forth in dance, that universally admired recreation, there was little parade and show. As far as our observations extended, we have never seen a Christmas day pass off more harmoniously. And, with all our ultra notions about holidays, we saw nothing that we particularly objected to.

—*Deseret News*

1856

December 25 (Spanish Fork, Utah)

Christmas Eve came and my darlings, with childish faith, hung up their stockings, wondering if Santa Claus would fill them. With aching heart, which I concealed from them, I assured them they would not be forgotten; and they fell asleep with joyful anticipations for the morning.

Not having a particle of sweetening, I knew not what to do. They must not, however, be disappointed. I then thought of some squash in the house which I boiled, then strained off the liquid, that, when simmered a few hours, made a sweet syrup. With this, and a little spice, I made gingerbread dough, which, when cut into every conceivable variety of design, and baked in a skillet, (I had no stove) filled their stockings and pleased them as much as would the most fancy confections.

—Hannah Last Cornaby
Autobiography and Poems

December (with the Martin Handcart Company in Wyoming)

It was supper time and we were hungry and without food, when a good brother came to our campfire. He asked if mother had no husband and she told him her husband had died two months ago and was buried on the Plains. The brother had been standing with his hands behind him. He then handed us a nice piece of beef to cook for supper. He left and came back with a beef bone and said, "Here is a bone to make some soup, and don't quarrel over it." Mother said, "Oh brother, we never quarrel over short rations, but we are very thankful to you for giving us this meat, as we do not have any and have not expected any."

—Patience Loader Rozsa Archer
"Recollections of the Past"

1857

December (Salt Lake Valley)

Sunday, 20th —at home
Monday, 21st —thrashing
Tuesday, 22nd —thrashed wheat
Wednesday, 23rd —cleaned up wheat
Thursday, 24th —cleaned wheat
Friday, 25th —Christmas, went to Farmington and went two miles below for clay to whitewash my houses.

—Levi Thornton
Diary

Christmas Is for Children

December 17, 1898

Christmas shoppers were strongly in evidence on the streets today. They were by no means confined to residents of Salt Lake City, but there were more than the usual Saturday visitors from the country. Delightedly gazing at the decorated windows of the business houses, the little folks, accompanying their parents or big sister, constituted a beautiful picture of happy expectancy.

One little tot, rapturously clasping her little "pudding" hands, while her eyes devoured a beautifully dressed doll in a toy shop window, exclaimed to her companions, "Oh, I mustn't look at it; I'm afraid I might want it."

A little chap with a face that looked like a fat dumpling with a hole cut into it, pointed a dirty little sausage-finger at a big hobby horse and gurgled out, "Golly!"

In order to deliver all the "things," including lumps of coal and bad potatoes for disobedient little boys and girls, Santa Claus will be compelled to use a very large sleigh, and so many reindeer to draw it that the music of the bells they wear will fill the whole world; and their Papa's and Mama's hearts will leap with joy at the bubbling happiness of their little ones.

—*Deseret Evening News*

(Willow Creek, Idaho)

James A. Smith and his wife, Annie Sellars Smith, left their home in Utah and settled in Willow Creek, about twelve miles northeast of Idaho Falls, in 1886. Their eight-year-old daughter, Mamie, took a special interest in her younger sister, Clara, and the two played together endlessly. Mamie was heartbroken this Christmas to think that little Clara would not get a doll. The little family was snowbound and their Christmas celebration would consist of homemade candy, apples, a cheerful fire and music.

Christmas morning found a little doll, neatly and beautifully dressed in her little sister's stocking. Mamie had taken a long clothespin from her mother's peg sack and had spent hours in hemming, folding, dyeing, tieing, painting and padding a doll for Clara so her Christmas cry in the morning would be one of gladness, not of disappointment. Clara Smith DeMott always cherished the memory of her first doll and of the happiness it brought and the never-to-be-forgotten loving sister who made her first doll from a clothespin.

—Deon Smith Seedall
Treasures of Pioneer History 4:201-2

One Christmas when I was a small girl, I had been wanting a doll with hair. I don't know how mother managed to get it, perhaps when they sold some dried peaches or walnuts to a store in St. George. Mother was so thrilled about it she couldn't wait until Christmas morning, so when I awakened in the night, she put my hand in a paper sack and said to guess what was there. I felt, and said, "It's got feathers on, it's a chicken." I couldn't guess what it was. The next morning when I looked into my stocking,

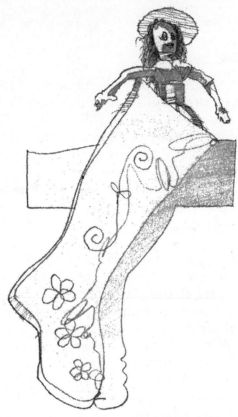

which was usually filled with English walnuts, hard tack candy, and an orange, I found the cutest little china doll with hair on a china head, arms, legs of china and a cloth body. I loved that little doll and kept it for years.

—Rose Ann G. Hafen
Treasures of Pioneer History 1 (1952):113-14

(Ephraim, Utah)

One Christmas Eve, two little pioneer girls hung up their homemade wool stockings in front of the fireplace, and then went to bed. Early the next morning, they rushed downstairs to see what Santa had brought them. They both wanted a pretty mug. When one of the girls looked in her stocking, she saw the mug and was very happy. When her sister looked in her stocking, she could only see an apple and a fried cake. She was so disgusted she said, "Such darn partiality," but she decided to take out the apple and see what else there might be, maybe some stick candy or something. In the bottom, she found the mug, and was so happy she forgave Santa Claus.

—Sarah D. Jensen
Treasures of Pioneer History 1 (1952):121

About 1885 (Elko, Nevada)

A schoolmistress had prepared a wonderful holiday program for her students. Everyone in town had contributed something to the event. There was a large Christmas tree decorated with popcorn, apples, doughnuts, and also a pack for Santa Claus to distribute among the school-children.

The crowd had all gathered but the duly appointed Santa Claus had not put in his appearance. Just at this crucial moment sleighbells were heard in the distance— they grew louder and louder. The teacher, looking out of the back door, saw a sleigh drawn by a beautiful span of horses, covered with snow and icicles, coming toward her. Around the girth of each horse was a string of shining silver bells. When the sleigh came to a halt, a man dressed for this sub-zero climate in cap, coat and long woolen chaps arose from the covers. It was George Badger, a kindly man who was foreman of the McIntyre Ranch in Elko, traveling to his home in Holden, Utah, after the last cattle roundup of the season.

George was immediately drafted into service. It took no persuasion on his part, and but little make-up for him to enter wholeheartedly into the spirit of the occasion. In seconds he turned his cap and coat wool side out and draped a string of bells around him. The entire school of youngsters arose with shouts of glee as this new Santa entered the door with his pack. How their faces glowed when their names were called and presents were handed to them by this strange and jovial Santa Claus. After the children had gone, the profuse thanks of the little teacher was sufficient reward for the help he had so willingly given. Then out into the cold night, with stars gleaming on the glistening snow, he continued his course to his ranch where he found the ranch boys snugly asleep in their warm beds.

—As told by the son of George Badger,
Franklin Badger of Holden, Utah
Treasures of Pioneer History 3 (1954):168-69

December 25, 1903 (Santa Clara, Utah)

One Christmas stands out in my mind above all others. It was the year 1903 and all our town was visited with a terrible epidemic of typhoid fever. Several were often down in a single family with the dread disease. There were many deaths in town.

There wasn't any money brought in that summer for our family, and the garden went to weeds. It was all the well ones could do to take care of the sick. Mother washed every day, and father watched by the bedsides with the exception of taking time off to do chores.

As Christmas grew near, Mother knew we wouldn't have a very good Christmas. When we knelt by her knee at bedtime to say our prayers, she reminded us to pray that we might have a happy Christmas. I prayed secretly that I might get a doll.

When Christmas morning finally arrived, it looked as though our prayers hadn't been answered. After breakfast, Leda Hafen came over to see what we had gotten for Christmas, and seeing that we had nothing she told her grandma Hafen who owned a store about it. Mrs. Hafen and her son Ernest went into the store and prepared gifts

for all of us. There was an alligator which wound up for
Ensign, a fancy work box for Ida, a doll each for Alice and
me, and marbles for the little brothers, Emil and Samuel.
Our Christmas turned out to be a happy one after all.

—Rose Ann G. Hafen
Treasures of Pioneer History 1 (1952):113-14

December 25, 1885

It was Christmas morning at 4 a.m. in the year 1885.
The ground was covered with snow and the moon was
shining very bright. My brothers, Willy, Jesse and I, thinking it was morning, got out of bed to see if old Santa Claus
had been there and found our stockings that were tacked
to the window sill. We were all thrilled to see that he had
come and had filled our stockings. I found my first big
doll and a small jewel box. The lid had a little Red Riding
Hood figure with the big gray wolf attached to it. The boys
found a tool box, and the baby found a little toy horse
with a cart fastened to it—when the wheels went round a
bell would ring. He would run and play with it and then
we would all run with him.

We decided we would take our baby brother for a ride
in the snow. We went out in our nightgowns and took
turns riding on mother's rocking chair—one pushing the
other. Mother prized the chair very much. It was made by
Stephen C. Perry—an early pioneer. The wind began to
blow and we were cold, so we went inside and enjoyed
eating candy and nuts; then we began to run and play
around mother's kitchen stove. As we were running, my
baby brother (two and a half years old) fell and cut his
forehead on the bench. Mother woke up, bandaged his
head, and put us all to bed until morning.

—Ariel Warren Perry
Treasures of Pioneer History 1 (1952):115

(Teton Valley, Wyoming)

Christmas was near and my father, F. W. Morgan, was to leave on the morrow, Dec. 22nd, for Market Lake, a distance of sixty miles, to bring back the sixty gallon barrel containing all our Christmas treasures. The barrel never failed to come in the four Christmases we had lived in the Basin.

Grandfather worked in the ZCMI in Salt Lake City and each year he and grandmother packed the barrel with apples, oranges, candy, nuts, raisins, currants, peel, toys for each of the children, and often clothing, and sent it to Market Lake where father went by team to get it. With money as scarce as it was and the stores as poorly stocked for Christmas as they were, the barrel was a veritable treasure chest.

The first two days father was gone passed rather slowly, but the third day actually dragged. From our low west window of our two-roomed log cabin, we could watch the winding road as it came up over the hill. Here, we spent most of the day with our noses pressed flat against the window-pane, watching for some sight of the sleigh.

As evening came, no sign of father, and mother became really worried. However, she put on a brave front, never letting us know how she felt. Finally, unable to stay awake any longer, we hung up our stockings and went to bed. Mother made a few cookies with raisin faces and hung them on the tree. She covered walnut shells with a few bits of tinsel she found. She cut raisin boxes in half and covered them with bits of crepe paper and wall paper and hung them on the tree. In each stocking she put a cookie or two and some covered walnut shells. Towards morning, she went to bed but not to sleep.

In the meantime, father had reached Market Lake in good time and had gone directly to the depot for the barrel, but he was told nothing had come for him. He decided it would surely come the next day, but the train came, bringing no barrel. The following day being Christmas, father spent hours walking the floor and thinking of mother at home with five sadly disappointed little youngsters. The day after Christmas failed to bring the barrel, so he went over to the little branch store and there was the barrel. He learned that it had been in for four days. It had been sent to F. W. Morgan, in care of the ZCMI branch store. Needless to say, he was not long in getting started for home.

Santa made up to us children on New Year's morning what he had failed to do on Christmas, and while we will never forget that Christmas, it was much more indelibly stamped on the minds of our parents.

—Alice Morgan Hansen
Treasures of Pioneer History 3 (1954):175-76

December 24, 1903 (Stettin, Germany)

After supper Bro. Smith was called to visit a family. While he was gone, the peculiar coincident, Santa Claus came, old and bent, and with long white hair and beard, but very pleasant. He asked the children if they could pray. When he had the proof that they could, he presented them with a fine parcel.

—Roy Anson Welker
Diary

December 25, 1916 (Bountiful, Utah)

I remember rushing down Christmas morning racing straight to my bulging stocking hanging from the mantel. As I pulled out an orange and a candy-cane, I reached far into the toe for the hard, round bulge, and there it was: a can of Eagle Brand milk. On my first Eagle Brand Christmas it was a new taste for me, but ever after I always asked Santa for a can of Eagle Brand milk. Father cut off the lid with the can opener and I was allowed to spoon it out, a little every day. What sweetness! Just like candy! Better than candy! It was so expensive, we could only afford it once a year. It was not Christmas for me now without my can of Eagle Brand milk!

Helen Richards Gardner
Letter to Susan Arrington Madsen

Sadness at Christmas

On Christmas Eve in the late 1860s, a tall gawkish young man from Pine Valley called to see if he could get a partner for the dance. My sister was already engaged to go, but in sympathy for the young man, she told him that I would accompany him. I was angry, but mother came to her aid. I repented and we all set off together.

The evening would have been a perfect pleasure but for the fact that some of the belles of the party made fun of my partner. I hid myself in shame in the corner by the fireplace and behind the onlookers—and when he went out with the mischievous boys and took too much "valley tan" whiskey I could not keep the tears back and I stole out unobserved and ran home to have a good cry.

—Martha Cragun Cox
Journal

December 1856 (Wyoming)

When we found the Saints [in the Martin and Willie Handcart Companies] they were destitute of the comforts of life. We found them in snow drifts badly frozen. We took them up in our wagons and made them as comfortable as possible but many died after we got them in our wagons. Many had died before we got to them. This was the most horrible sight I ever saw. Many who went out to meet them were also badly frozen. We got home after 35 days travel, in all traveling seven hundred miles. We got home (to the Salt Lake Valley) about Christmastime. The Saints in the Valley thought that we were perhaps frozen in the mountains for the snow was very deep and it was very cold. A great many froze their feet and some their noses but the hand of the Lord was over us and we got home safe. Found my family all well, lost nothing except my flax which stayed in water too long and spoiled. This was a considerable loss.

—Levi Thornton (member of the group of volunteers
sent by Brigham Young to rescue
the handcart pioneers stranded in Wyoming)

For Christmas, a beloved aunt from Provo had sent my mother, Lucy Potter Blackham, a beautiful doll dressed in a taffeta gown. Every child in the town knew about it long before daylight Christmas morning as it was the custom to go from one house to another calling "Christmas Gift," and see what the other children had received. Her beautiful doll was a great curiosity, especially to her baby brother who wanted it badly. To hush his cries, she hid the doll in the oven of their old-fashioned stove. In the meantime, her father arose and made a big fire in the stove. She said she knew it was her punishment from the Lord for being selfish with her baby brother when they found the doll in the oven burned to a crisp. She mourned for two weeks over the loss of the beautiful doll.

—Mella Morley
Treasures of Pioneer History 3 (1954):143-44

December 25, 1888 (Franklin, Idaho)

When I was about seven, my Grandmother Lowe gave me a lovely wax doll with yellow curls and a pretty lacy dress. Wax dolls were a luxury in those days, so it was carefully wrapped and laid away in the bureau drawer, only to be looked at once in a while. Each day I would take it from its hiding place and admire its beauty, then carefully lay it back again. One day when I went to admire my beautiful doll, I found a great tragedy had befallen it. Its pretty face was all scratched and disfigured. My younger brother had found the doll's hiding place and had scraped all the wax from its face for chewing gum! I was so heart-broken I couldn't get over it for days!

—Ada Lowe Hart
Cache Valley Newsletter, Dec. 1972

(Gentile Valley, Idaho)

Throughout the day, every child's eye had been on the "community Christmas tree." And long before the day was over, every child had set his heart upon a special one of the gifts that hung from its drooping branches, eagerly hoping it to be the very one to which Santa had attached his name.

How vividly I still remember the big, bright-eyed doll with flaxen hair that was so beautifully dressed and was propped high in the branches of the tinseled tree. How well I remember the longing of my childish heart to hold it in my arms and claim it for my very own.

Suddenly, I realized that my name was being called out. Shifting my gaze from the adorable object to the one Santa held in his hand, I beheld a small purse encased in pearls with blue forget-me-nots painted on one side, and hanging from a silver chain. Though a small gift, it was a lovely one, and might have been the very one of my choice

had my heart not been already set on the beautiful doll. After claiming my gift, as I walked back to my place close by my mother, yet unable to release my cherished hope, I sidled close and whispered shyly in her ear, "Is the purse all Santa has for me?"

No doubt, through her motherly instinct, she had sensed my longing desire. And no doubt the same keen pain that pierced my heart pierced hers also. Drawing me tenderly to her, she kissed my forehead and breathed softly, "Yes, dear, the little purse is all."

—Lydia Bennett Egbert
Personal History

About 1865-70 (Moberley, England)

Father Christmas was an eccentric fellow, thin and tall, with a long, straggly beard, wearing a stove-pipe hat and carrying a long, lean bag. Father Christmas was always engaged to come and distribute gifts to the children, but he was very exacting concerning the past behavior of each child. He always conducted a "questionnaire" first, as to the child's worthiness of receiving a gift. Sometimes they would receive a rap on the knuckles and he was even known to give a child a lash with a whip if he knew something about the child not to his credit. He would say: "Why did you not curtsy to the schoolmaster last summer when you met him on the turn-pike road?" or "Were you among the children who were singing ungodly songs on the Sabbath?" or again, "Can you tell me the text of the sermon a fortnight ago?"

Then satisfied, he would distribute the sweets in his bag as he saw fit. My brother Joseph and my sister Mary Hannah and I had no love for Father Christmas for he had a long memory of past offenses.

—Sarah Jane Starkey
Treasures of Pioneer History 4 (1955):198

December 25, 1890 (Caroline Madsen, Fairview Utah, re-
ceived a letter on Christmas day from her husband, Hans
Madsen, who was serving a mission in New Zealand. The
couple's first and only child, Leona, had died a little more
than a month earlier, and Hans had not yet received word)

Christmas Day. Oh a sad day for me. I got a letter from
Hans and he writes so much about the baby, not knowing
she is dead. I went with ma down to Sister Neilson's for
dinner, read letters to all that was there. Went to the
dance awhile and looked on.

—Caroline Christensen Madsen
Journal

(Oak Creek, Utah)

December 24, 1879: Weather colder than ever, the
dough freezes to the pan while we were mixing it.

December 25, 1879: Christmas. Not a merry one for I
can not think of any thing but the cold and my friends
who are camped on the banks of the Colorado River without houses or tents and exposed to the inclemency of the
weather. May the Lord preserve them from suffering is
my prayer continually.

December 26, 1879: How changed is my situation now
from what it was last Christmas. Then, the baby's mother
was alone while all the rest of the household had gone to
the Christmas party. Now, she sleeps in the grave and her
baby is left to keep me company in her stead. Yesterday
Br. George Lovell brought me some wood on his shoulders
from his place as he saw I was out. Wrote to my friends on
the Colorado (River).

—Eliza Marie Partridge Lyman
Diary

December 25, 1862

All of us children hung up our stockings Christmas eve. We jumped up early in the morning to see what Santa had brought, but there was not a thing in them. Mother wept bitterly. She went to her box and got a little apple and cut it in little tiny pieces and that was our Christmas. But, I have never forgotten how I loved her dear hands as she was cutting that apple.

—Hannah Daphne Smith Dalton
Autobiography, Church Archives

December 25, 1903 (Salt Lake City, Utah)

My regular monthly allowance from my husband was $25.00, which required strict budgeting to make it cover rent, food, clothes, and incidentals. So, for Christmas he sent an extra $10.00, which looked like a fortune to us. We decided that even if we were alone, and very lonely, we would enjoy a real Christmas.

We didn't aspire to roast turkey, but we did plan for roast chicken, plum pudding, cranberry sauce, and all the trimmings. We would have a tiny tree for the baby and toys galore, and presents for each other. What fun we had trying to decide which of our many needs we wanted most!

But alas! Before we had time to execute any of our cherished plans, Aunt Julina came down one night and asked if we couldn't just as well pay the rent before Christmas as to wait until the first of the month! Imagine if you can, our disappointment! Ella looked at me, and I at her, out hearts sank, and tears came to our eyes. But, without a word, I swallowed the lump in my throat, went to my purse and handed her over the $10.00—every cent we had in the house! Of course, anyone can use an extra ten at Christmastime!

As a result, our Christmas dinner consisted of boiled rice, canned tomatoes, and whatever else we happened to have in the house, without trimmings. Tears rolled down our cheeks as we sat down to the humble fare, and while we offered thanks and were grateful for even that, we felt just a little hard in our hearts at the inequality of things.

We never discussed the incident later in our lives without crying—even thirty years later. But we can now laugh amid our tears, which we could not do then.

—Mary (Mamie) Woolley Chamberlain
Autobiography

December 25, about 1896 (Snowflake, Arizona)

I remember the poorest Christmas I ever spent. Mother had managed in some way to make us three older girls a Christmas dress and we went to a Christmas party at the Church house. We were given a few pieces of candy each and decided to save them and take them home to the four little boys. Emma and I saved ours, but Kate ate part of hers. We scolded her all the way home. It was all the boys would get for Christmas. Upon our arrival home, Leonard said, "I hope Santa Claus won't always be this poor."

—Mary Hulet Coburn
Journal

December 25, 1900

The children had to wait till I had a fire made, then they all marched down according to age. How happy the children were with their presents. At eight o'clock, I was called down to administer to Brother Barratt but when I got there he had just expired. I spent an hour or more with Sister Barratt and Sister Watson trying to comfort them . . . administered to Sister Barratt.

—Anthon H. Lund
(Church historian, 1900-1921)
Diary

December 25, 1851 (Nephi, Utah)

Isaac and Elizabeth Grace were among the first to settle in Nephi, Utah, arriving in October 1851. A few days after they arrived, the Charles Sperry family arrived to become their first neighbors.

Before building a home for his own family, Isaac built one for his sister, and then helped the other brethren build theirs, they in turn helped him. Charles Sperry helped by making mud adobe for a chimney. It was freezing weather and they were hurrying to complete it for Christmas. They discovered that the mortar had frozen, and that if a fire was made in the fireplace, it would help to dry it out. So, on Christmas day they moved into their snug little log cabin. Everyone was merry as the Christmas dinner was cooking in the new fireplace—when an awful crash came. The frozen chimney came all to pieces and fell all over the room. With tears in her eyes, Elizabeth picked up her babies and went back to her wagon. The incident of the chimney was a sad blow, but with pluck and energy they built it again with planks and mud. It stood until they could do better.

—Florence McCune Lunt
Treasures of Pioneer History 1 (1952):112

Missionaries and Servicemen

December 25, 1840

Christmas day in London. The Church bells throughout the city commenced chanting for meeting at half past ten. We met with the Saints . . . at 11 o'clock and we taught the Saints some plain principles, which had a good effect. We took our Christmas dinner with Br. Morgan. He had his family at home with him. The dinner consisted of Baked Mutton, Goose, Rabbit Pies, Minced Pies, and Plum Pudding, and bread and cheese, Porter and water. We spent the evening at Mr. Albums in conversing about the things of God. This was the first Christmas I have spent in England. Where I shall be next Christmas day the Lord only knows. May the Lord preserve my life, my wife and child in peace I pray, and enable all the Saints to be established in righteousness.

—Wilford Woodruff
Diary

December 25, 1853 (Luapahoehoe, Hawaii)

In the afternoon we got the privilege to preach in a Calvinist Meeting House to quite a large congregation of natives. I don't find it any different with the natives than any other class of people. They manifest the same spirits: . . . some believe, and some fight and oppose it, and others obey it, the same as it is among all people. We baptized three this afternoon.

—Thomas Karren
Journal

December 25, 1878 (England)

Runcorn, Cheshire . . . an abundance of earthly bounties (for Christmas dinner) such as plum pudding and mince pies, and a fat goose weighing 10½ pounds.

—James Lovett Bunting
Journal

December 25, 1851 (Tubuai, South Sea Islands)

The native women and children went about making preparations for (their first) Christmas celebration. They took sand and scoured all the benches and floor. To decorate the room, they placed Ito trees of the most vivid green, which reached almost to the roof. On these trees they placed tea leaves made into wreaths by the women, which added a bright color and a pleasing fragrance. They then hung pictures of the Prophet Joseph Smith and his brother Hyrum amid beautiful flowers of the bauran tree.

Then came dinner. Pigs weighing 100 pounds each were roasted whole. There was plenty of wild chickens and fish of all kinds. There was poi, bread fruit, coconuts, pineapples, bananas and many kinds of native fruit. The milk from the coconuts was used for beverage. Each article of food was wrapped in large leaves and piled in a heap, resembling a haystack for ready use. Mats were spread for seats. Leaves woven together made the tablecloth. Franklin Gouard blessed the food and offered thanks. After dinner we held a religious service.

As I gazed at the scenery (as evening came), beautiful beyond description, the tall stately coconut trees, the roar of the mighty ocean, it seemed I must be in a different world entirely from the one in which my parents and all my relatives, save those with me, lived, wrapped in ice and snow, as I knew they would be this day. But I knew of their love and that their hearts glowed with the love of the lowly Master and the Spirit of Christmas.

—Adapted from Louisa Barnes Pratt
(first sister missionary for the Church)
Heart Throbs of the West 8 (1947):189-398

December 25, 1840

Birmingham, Lane End, England. Friday, 25th, attended conference with the Church. Had a good time, gave the Church much instruction. Found Elder G. A. Smith not very well. Stayed night with him at Br. Samuel Johnsons.

—Brigham Young
Journal

December 25, 1852 (Fredrikstad Jail, Norway. Twenty-one-year-old Christian J. Larsen, a Dane, presided over Latter-day Saint missionary work in Norway. He had been jailed since October 15 with fellow Danish, Swedish, and Norwegian Latter-day Saints for unauthorized performance of religious ordinances.)

Eight of the Saints were permitted to come in to [see] us in our room, and we enjoyed ourselves together with song and prayer, as well as in conversation. Later in the day I, in company with Elder Ahmanson, Svend Larsen and J. A. Jensen, were permitted to go out visiting. I and

Bro. Larsen spent quite a while with Carl Widerborg and afterwards joined us at a place called "Trara," where quite a number of the Saints had assembled. The pastoral letter, which I had written to the Saints, was read, and all seemed to appreciate its contents and to rejoice and it was indeed a Day of Liberty, especially so to us prisoners. Later, our guard, Mr. Billington, took us back to the city and out to Vaterland, where we met with some of the Saints that lived in that neighborhood and we had, again, a very enjoyable time with them. Elder S. Larsen, on that occasion, blessed the child of Brother S. P. Larsen, naming it: Gabrielle Jessie Larsen. From there we went to our prison-hotel.

—Christian J. Larsen
Journal

December 25, 1892 (New Zealand)

This morning I was up early and got my white shirt which had been washed and ironed by Sottie.

A resolution was passed last evening that we were not to open our socks until the first bell had rung. This being the case, I wore one of Bro. S. C. R.'s socks until the bell rang. Old Santa Claus was very good to me, as my sock contained a rotten potato and a lot of shells. I fasted that I may have a good time and that the girls may be preserved from all evil. The Xmas dinner was a fine one consisting of potatoes, new and old, soup, meat fresh and putrid, nice bread, a bit of butter, cakes, biscuits and lollies.

—Hans Madsen
Journal

December 24-25, 1874 (Halmstad, Sweden)

Christmas eve we decorated our hall and made preparations for the approaching Christmas festivity. Christmas day. . we had ottensång (special early-morning services), many people and quite a good spirit prevailed. Bro. G. Gunnarsson invited the Saints to his home in the evening and we had a very pleasant time. I was presented by them with some Christmas presents: 5 kronor [money], from Sister Hulta Östergre, a scarf from a Sister Maria, 3 handkerchiefs from Sister Betty, and 50 øre [money] from Sister Melia.

—Carl Arvid Carlquist
Journal

December 24-25, 1852 (on the Atlantic Ocean—Elder Edward Stevenson was among a group of missionaries who spent Christmas on a sailboat on their way to serve in Gibraltar)

This is a Christmas that I will not soon forget. [The ocean] is rougher than is common and it is about as much as we can do to keep in our berths. Heavy waves often come over the top of the ship. The waves look like mountains heaving. It looks sometimes as though the ship, when going over a large wave, is going to plunge under, but rises with the next.

Perrigrine Sessions was thrown on a provision box and took a ride from one side to the other and back while a woman was thrown down, taking a slide across. Many laughed and some were somewhat alarmed.

Christmas eve we agreed to keep this day as a day of fasting and prayer. Towards evening the roughness abated. Having kept up our fast, we took some supper. With the aid of Brother Nathan Porter, my right hand man, who has been blest with less seasickness than most of us, I got our supper, a currant pudding and some short cake, which we divided with those that are the most sick, which they said was first rate. This ended our Christmas.

—Edward Stevenson
Journal

December 1857 (Vejle, Denmark)

It is the first day of Christmas. I stayed here and observed a fast day. There was a meeting in Brother C. P. Stiep's house, but few came because there was heavy rain and storm.

—Peter Nielsen
Journal

December 24, 1892 (New Zealand)

Christmas eve was quite a treat. Having thrown all the cares of the mission to one side, we voted to have a good time and the following will give you a slight idea how our happy eve passed:

B. Goddard, chairman or toastmaster

Monroe Hixon: song
C. W. Taylor: Christmas stories
Ed. J. Palmer: song
Wm. T. Steward: Christmas address
Hans Madsen: song
Ed. Atking: song
Presentation of socks by Santa Claus: Milton Bennion
Jn. G. Kelson: song
Jno. M. Hendry, toast: Our wives and sweethearts
Jas. S. Abbott: Toast, sweethearts
R. G. Meikle: Toast, wives
Hendry: song, "Where did you get that hat?"
C. B. Bartlett: toast
Milton Bennion: song
Oscar Andrews: song
Wm. Douglass, Jr: Toast. Christmas, the present
L. C. Rasmussen: song, Danish
"Home Sweet Home" by the jolly party

General hand-shaking and wishing each other A Merry
    Christmas
The Star Spangled Banner by the jolly party
    The above program kept us up until after midnight,
but we did nothing whatsoever of which to be sorry. All
sport was innocently participated in and with the spirit of
kindness.

—Hans Madsen
Journal

December 25, 1846 (with the Mormon Battalion, marching
through the Arizona desert on the way to San Diego)

    Christmas. Left the Pemoes [Pimas]. Traveled twenty
miles and camped without water. Traveled through a
sandy desert. Ate our Christmas supper by the roadside.
Had cold beans, pancakes, and pumpkin sauce.

—Miles Thompson, Private, Company D
Diary

December 25, 1846 (with the Mormon Battalion)

    This is rather a strange Christmas to me. My life with
my family in days gone by was called to mind and con-
trasted with my present situation on the sandy deserts
through which pass the Gila and Colorado rivers. Suffering much at times for want of water, but still pressing forward with parched lips, scalded shoulders, weary limbs,
blistered feet, worn out shoes, and ragged clothes. But
with me the prospect of the result of my present toils
cheers me on.

—William Hyde, Second Orderly Sergeant, Company B
Diary

December 25, 1846 (with the Mormon Battalion)

I wish I could call this a Merry Christmas. I confess it is as melancholy a one as I have ever experienced. Not a green bush to attract the eye. Not a sleigh bell to please the ear. Not anyone to greet us with, "I wish you a Merry Christmas." Instead, all around us is a sandy thirsty plain, covered here and there with patches of ill-looking shrubbery.

—Guy M. Keysor, Private, Company B
Diary

December 1862 (with Union forces in Washington, D.C.)

John said the men will have to go to battle before many weeks and this will be the last Christmas that many of us will live to see. . . I told him I would do my best to help get the dinner for these poor men if he would let some of the men help me. He said you can have all the help you need, and the men will be glad to come and help you. 'Tell me what you want for dinner,' I asked. He said he would like turkey, roast beef, pork, vegetables, plum pudding, and mince pie. I made seven puddings for the company and twenty-five pies. The cakes and fruit we bought. . . . At twelve o'clock on Christmas day, the table was set for the whole company and the men sat down to a fine dinner. It was the last Christmas dinner for many of those poor men, for nearly all of Company E, 10th Infantry, fell in battle the following March.

—Patience Loader Rozsa Archer, wife of First Sergeant John
Rozsa, converted to Mormonism in 1858 while in Utah with the
Utah Expedition [Johnston's Army]
Journal

Christmas Is a Family Time

(LDS Church Ranch, Kanab, Utah)

Father had ordered a nice Christmas for all, including toys and trinkets for the little tots, shoes, suits, and overcoats for the older ones, but the snow came and all the mail was unable to get through. This was a great disappointment to father, as he had counted on making all so happy.

In the face of this difficulty, he decided not to be outdone. So, as soon as the children were up, he met us, dressed in a big fur coat, a long white beard made of angora goat hair to represent Santa, a long string of sleigh bells over his shoulders, and stamping his feet and rubbing his hands together before the big pitch fire. He explained to us that the snow was so deep that he had to leave his "pack" but had to come to take us all for a merry sleigh ride. This so delighted us that we did not miss the presents. We all went except Mother who remained to prepare a good Christmas plum pudding which we all enjoyed after the long ride through the frosty air. The breath of the horses froze and formed icicles all around their nostrils, as we drove through the fields and over fences on the crusted snow.

We called on each of the neighbors to wish them good cheer and we considered it one of the very best Christmas days we had ever enjoyed!

—Mary "Mamie" Woolley Chamberlain
Autobiography

December 25, 1860 (Bountiful, Utah)

The Cyrus Page family had just built their home and were very low on funds, so they thought the children were small and wouldn't notice if Santa didn't come and they said nothing about it. Our grandmother Susan Ashby Page cooked the best she could with what she had and made little pies and cakes and some molasses candy.

When the children got up the next morning, they looked at one another and couldn't keep the tears back. Grandfather Cyrus went out, jumped on his bally horse and rode down to the settlement to Jonnie Thurgood's store and made a bargain with him to take a barrell of molasses. He bought some candy and nuts and a toy for each of the children, also a present for Grandmother. He said that would be the last Christmas Eve that would find him unprepared for Santa, and it was.

—History of Cyrus Page
Our Pioneer Heritage 16 (1973):179

December 25, about 1880 (American Fork, Utah)

Our Christmases were delightful and full of joy. Not a house full of gifts, but a toy for each, a small doll, maybe an orange and homemade cookies to dig in one's stocking for; a sumptuous dinner with mother's plum pudding and mince pies. Raisins on the stems were sprinkled with brandy, then a match set fire to them and we would see who could grab the most from the dish. Nuts were scattered on the floor for us to scramble for, and the candy hard tack. My that was great!

—Alice Ann Paxman (McCune)
Autobiography

As a child I lived in the little Mormon colony of Colonia Juarez in northern Mexico. Early one Christmas morning I was carrying a small bucket of milk to my grandmother's house, which was a few streets away, when I saw that a house through the block was on fire. It was the home of one of my friends. Terrified, I dashed home to tell my parents. They and all the neighbors rushed to help, but their best efforts could not save the house.

In those days people fastened real candles on the Christmas tree and lit them. In my friend's home one of the candles had tipped, setting first the tree and then the house ablaze. Everything was destroyed.

The community rallied around the family, supplying all their immediate needs. And I was even a bit jealous when the children of the family received more gifts for Christmas that year than had been under their tree.

I know the family would have been helped, whatever the time of year, but the outpouring of generosity seemed especially appropriate for Christmas Day, when traditionally we enjoy a special readiness to share.

—Camilla Eyring Kimball
from *Family Christmas Traditions*

Early 1900s (Ephraim, Utah)

The "Anderson tribe" took up about a city block in Ephriam. On one corner my father lived, across the road his sister lived, across the road west one of my uncles lived and half a block north was Grandmother and some other of the children.

Our Christmas celebration was a week long. The one who had all of us to their house at Christmas time was the leader and they would all bring pot luck. They'd all bring something. Then, the second night of the holidays we'd meet over to Aunt Sarah's, the third night to Aunt Maggie's, and the fourth night to Aunt Josie's. And so it went around for one week. No wonder we looked like pigs ourselves when we got through eating. All that food! That was the good Christmas time.

—Leland Anderson
Memoirs

(Circle Valley, Utah)

At a specific date in dead winter we had to be out of our snug little house so I started to build again with the few materials I had. Time did not allow me to build much of a house. So, I erected a small little house, eight by ten, to be used as a chicken coop after we built a better home. About Christmas we got our chicken coop finished and we moved in. There, we had our first Christmas dinner under our own roof and thanked God for the prosperity he had blessed us with, feeling sure things would be better in the future.

—Oluf Christian Larson
Autobiography

December 25, 1877

Christmas is over at last. The day so eagerly anticipated by the little folks. Owing to the decoration of the tree, Santa Claus had but little for their stockings. There were some cakes and apples and little prize boxes, and some trifles that Bessie had made for her brothers and sisters.

I sent the buggy for some of those invited to dinner. I did not care to invite those who had friends and good cheer at home, but remembered the poor and the lonely. About ten o'clock the band serenaded us. We had a nice dinner, I sent the old people home in a covered carriage it was snowing so fast.

I went with Myron to a ball at the Academy Hall. We enjoyed the music and dancing until eleven o'clock when we came home thoroughly tired and glad to close the day and sleep until the beams of another day should call us to life and action.

—Mary Jane Mount Tanner
A Fragment: Autobiography of Mary Jane Mount Tanner

December 25, 1841 (Nauvoo, Illinois)

Christmas Eve. Visited and dined at Hiram Kimball's with B. Young, H.C. Kimball, O. Pratt, W. Woodruff, J. Taylor and wives. Hiram Kimball gave each of the Twelve a lot of land, and supper of turkey.

—Willard Richards
Diary

December 25, 1870 (Salt Lake City)

Yesterday I saw about rooms for Sister Stevenson (a new immigrant from England), and she moved to them in the afternoon. I loaned her a fancy dwarf stove, two joints of pipe and elbows, a kettle and frying pan, and gave her about a bushel of potatoes, a nice piece of beef, some molasses, flour, three scuttles of coal, one candle and candlestick, and in the evening my son Brigham brought her a basket of provisions from the contributions to the poor.

—Albert Carrington, Church historian, 1870-1874
Diary

(At the home of Mary and Peter Sorenson, Swedish immigrants, Holladay, Utah)

The tree was alight with colored candles, but not for long; it was too dangerous. Everyone held hands and danced around the tree, singing the Christmas songs we knew. We little ones would try to get a glance at what Santa had left us, and Grandma would sit in her rocking chair and watch, laughing and crying at the same time. I always got a doll, perfume, hair ribbon and a hanky.

Christmas morning about ten or eleven o'clock, Grandma would call us in to have "Dop-a-greet-ta." In English this means a big bowl of tasty soup, some meat, and a plate of bread. We each had a saucer. The blessing was asked, then each took a piece of bread, dipped it in the soup, holding the saucer under so as not to spill it as we took it to our mouths. Mother said it was to represent the Last Supper.

—Leah Waters
Our Pioneer Heritage 13 (1970):188

(Tooele)

A family dinner was always held in Tooele at the home of pioneer Andrew J. Johnson. The long kitchen table would seat 24 people and was often filled twice on Christmas day.

All of the grownups would sit down to eat first, the meal being served in the middle of the afternoon. The older girls waited on tables while the younger children played outside. Elof, when asking the blessing, would pray for what seemed an eternity to the younger children, peeking in doors and windows. Numerous trips to the kitchen would be made by the youngsters, hopefully waiting for the grownups to finish.

The meal usually consisted of roast pork, stewed chicken, dried beans, dried corn, potatoes, cabbage, plum pudding, and fruit cake.

—*The History of Tooele*

1890s (Perry [Thatcher], Idaho)

In our family, Christmas meant the merry tinkling of utensils mingled with happy voices resounding about the kitchen, the sweet, spicy aroma ascending from hot, steaming mince pies, fruitcake, and ginger cookies that were slid from the oven. Nuts and oranges and all of the other delicacies that came as a rare treat at that one glorious season of the year.

The first thrilling event occurred late in November when mother would bring out the brown glazed crock and the ingredients for grinding and assembling the mincemeat. In routine, too, came the mixing of the fruitcake and plum pudding—both must have time to properly age.

For each of these occasions, we children never failed to be on hand. No one ever attempted to shoo us from the kitchen. It was considered part of our Christmas joy and mother saw to it that we were never deprived of anything that would make us happy. It was exciting, indeed, when we all scrambled for a ringside view around the old kitchen table, eagerly watching, our watering little mouths all fixed for a pinch of raisins and nuts, a slice of candied fruit or a sprinkle of sweet spice in the palm of our hand.

—Lydia Bennett Egbert
Personal History

(Salt Lake City)

Christmas, 1883: Christmas came with all its fun and excitement. We enjoyed ourselves first class as usual. I had it in mind to mention what each one received as presents, but when I think that there were twenty-nine pairs of stockings hung up and all filled, I fear I should become weary of trying to mention all.

Christmas, 1887: We had one of the worst storms on Christmas Day I ever saw. It came up suddenly just as I

was getting dinner. The wind blew and the snow came into the kitchen and was so cold I could hardly get the things to cook, and what made it still worse I had two turkeys in Nett's stove and had to go back and forth to see them. But I don't get discouraged very easy, so I got the dinner on in good shape and all seemed to enjoy it, and by the laughing I could hear in the parlour, I think all had a good time.

I shall let pass all the tangled ends, vexations and ups and downs of the past year. Life is like a weaver's net, which has both bright and grey threads.

Christmas, 1889: I made a sacrifice of one of the greatest pleasures of my life, that is my family dinner on that day, but my family has outgrown my accommodations until I get a larger house. But the children all came in the evening so as to let me down easy.

Christmas, 1890: Christmas day is past. The children were all here except the missionary boys. We missed them beyond everything, but they are on a good cause. God bless them wherever they are.

—Rachel Emma Woolley Simmons, pioneer of 1847
Heart Throbs of the West 11 (1950):153, 208

December 25, 1867 (Manti, Utah)

When I was seven years old my sister Almeda lived across the street east, and a half block south from our home. She had a small dog named "Queen." It was a family pet.

Christmastime was approaching and I longed to do something to add to the pleasure of that good holiday which everybody looks forward to expecting some fine surprise. When I racked my little brain trying to think out some way of getting a small gift for each one of our family, I finally knew that such a thing could not be done; then I thought I must do something which would start the day out with laughter, so I caught Queen, the little dog, and with mother's measuring tape took the measure of the length and circumference of her body, and the measure around her neck and head.

I kept my plans a secret. I watched mother's sewing basket, and saw some white material which I thought was suited to my needs, and after some persuasion mother said "If you need it for something useful you can have it, but remember not to waste it because it is valuable."

My playhouse was in the attic, and there with needle, thread, the measuring tape and mother's best scissors I worked with a will until I had completed a hat and dress or body covering for Queen. The hat was made of a round piece of material gathered to fit Queen's head, with a ruffle almost two inches wide encircling the hat, tape and strings to tie it securely under her chin. (While making the outfit I was obliged to capture Queen and hold her down to fit the things to her body and head). Her dress was a complete covering for her back and sides, from neck to tail, with the two inch ruffle all around it and numerous matched tape strings to tie it underneath her neck, and body, and around each leg and her tail.

Bright and early Christmas morning while the family was dressing, I ran to my sister's home and got Queen, took her to my attic, and dressed her in her new costume. Oh what a comical sight she was, her little eyes filled with excitement peering out from under the ruffles of the white hat, and when I turned her loose in our living room she ran in circles, jumped in the air and almost turned summersalts trying to extricate herself from that costume. She barked and yelped while dancing around the floor with her ruffles waving in the air. The whole family roared with delight.

Someone came rushing from the outside and as the door opened Queen gave a leap and went bounding over the snow in double quick time. There was a cat-hole in my sister's door large enough for Queen to push through. She was through in a jiffy. As she ran home I followed closely behind. And as I came close to the house I heard the laughter of my sister and her husband. Queen was still dancing in her new suit, which was so securely tied she could not dislodge it. When my sister was able to control her laughter she said, "You young rascal, how could you think of doing such an unusual thing? Why, it's as good as a circus."

—Lorena Eugenia Washburn Larsen
Life Sketch

Bibliography

Primary Sources (Published)

Periodicals

Cache Valley Newsletter. Preston, Idaho, 1972.
Deseret News. Salt Lake City, 1850–1984.
Improvement Era. Salt Lake City, 1897–1970.
Juvenile Instructor. Salt Lake City, 1918.
Young Women's Journal. Salt Lake City, 1889–1914.

Personal Histories and Diaries

Chamberlain, Mary E. Woolley. *Mary E. Woolley Chamberlain: Handmaiden of the Lord, An Autobiography*. Salt Lake City [?]: Published by the Woolley family, 1981.

Dalton, Hannah Daphne Smith. Autobiography. *Pretty Is As Pretty Does*. Church Archives.

Kimball, Camilla Eyring. *Family Christmas Traditions*. Newport Beach, California: KenningHouse Publishing, 1982.

Pratt, Louisa Barnes. Autobiography. *Heart Throbs of the West* 8(1947):189-398.

Simmons, Rachel Emma Woolley. Diary. *Heart Throbs of the West* 11(1950):153-208.

Sorenson, Isaac. Autobiography. *Utah State Historical Quarterly* 24(1956):51-70.

Spencer, Clarissa Young, with Mabel Harmer. *Brigham Young At Home*. Salt Lake City: Deseret News Press, 1947.

Ward, Margery W., ed. *A Fragment: The Autobiography of Mary Jane Mount Tanner*. Salt Lake City: University of Utah Library, 1980.

Primary Sources (Unpublished)

Diaries, Journals, Autobiographies, and Other Contemporary Writings

Anderson, Leland. Memoirs. Typescript of oral interviews in possession of his family. Made available to the author by Shirley Anderson Cazier, Logan, Utah.

Archer, Patience Loader Rozsa. Autobiography. Typescript, Brigham Young University.

Bailey, Charles Ramsden. Autobiography. Holograph, Utah State University Special Collections.

Bliss, Robert Stanton. Diary. Microfilm of holograph, Church Archives.

Bullock, Thomas. Diary. Typescript, Church Archives.

Bunting, James Lovett. Diary. Holograph, Brigham Young University.

Carlquist, Carl Arvid. Autobiography. Typescript, Utah State University Special Collections.

Carrington, Albert. Diary. Holograph, University of Utah.

Coburn, Mary Hulet. Journal. Microfilm of holograph, Utah State University Special Collections.

Cox, Martha Cragun. Journal. Holograph, Church Archives.

Egbert, Lydia Bennett. Autobiography. Typescript privately distributed. Made available to the author by Ann Peterson, Hyrum, Utah.

Erickson, Hilda Andersson. Diary. Church Archives.

Gardner, Helen Richards. Letter to Susan Arrington Madsen, dated November 19, 1983.

Grant, Heber Jeddy. Diary. Holograph, Heber J. Grant Collection, Church Archives.

Historian's Office Journal. Church Archives.

Hyde, William. Journal. Holograph, Church Archives.

Journal History of the Church. A massive, day-by-day record of The Church of Jesus Christ of Latter-day Saints. Church Archives.

Karren, Thomas. Diary. Microfilm of holograph, Church Archives.

Keysor, Guy Messiah. Diary. Holograph, Church Archives.

Larsen, Christian J. Journal. Photocopy of transcript, Church Archives.

Larsen, Lorena E. Washburn. Life sketch. Typescript, Salt Lake Genealogical Library, Salt Lake City, Utah.

Larsen, Shauna Stewart. Transcript of taped memoirs. In possession of author.

Larson, Oluf Christian. Autobiography. Duplication of typescript, Church Archives.

Lund, Anthon Hendrik. Diary. Microfilm of holograph, Church Archives.

Lyman, Eliza Marie Partridge. Journal. Holograph, Church Archives.

Madsen, Caroline Christensen. Journal. Holograph, Church Archives.

Madsen, Hans. Journal. Holograph, Church Archives.

Nielsen, Peder (later known as Peter Nielson). Holograph, Church Archives.

Pearce, Jean Rio Baker. Diary. Typescript, Church Archives.

Richards, Willard. Diary. Holograph, Church Archives.

Salt Lake City Fourteenth Ward Minute Book. Church Archives.

San Bernardino Ward Historical Record. Church Archives.

Smith, George Albert. Diary. Microfilm of holograph, Church Archives.

Smith, George Albert. Papers. Special Collections, University of Utah.

Smith, Joseph, Jr. Diary. Holograph, Church Archives.

Stevenson, Edward. Journal. Microfilm of holograph, Church Archives.

Stout, Hosea. Diary. Holograph, Utah State Historical Society.

Thompson, Miles. Diary. Holograph, Church Archives.

Thornton, Levi. Journal. Typescript, Utah State University Special Collections.

Welker, Roy Anson. Diary. Holograph, Church Archives.

Wilson, Mary Jane Perkins. Autobiography. Transcript, Utah State University Special Collections.

Woodruff, Wilford. Journal. Holograph, Church Archives.

Wright, Angus Taylor. Autobiography. Transcript, Utah State University Special Collections.

Young, Brigham. Diary. Holograph and manuscript, Church Archives.

Secondary Sources (Published)

An Enduring Legacy. 6 vols. Salt Lake City: Daughters of Utah Pioneers, 1978-1983.

Arrington, Leonard J. Historical Christmas cards. Salt Lake City, privately published (1972-1983). Each card, published annually, has a separate title. Copies in possession of the author.

Arrington, Leonard J. and Davis Bitton. *Saints Without Halos: The Human Side of Mormon History.* Salt Lake City: Signature Books, 1982.

Arrington, Leonard J., and Susan Arrington Madsen. *Sunbonnet Sisters.* Salt Lake City: Bookcraft, 1984.

Carroll, Elsie Chamberlain, ed. *History of Kane County.* Salt Lake City: Daughters of Utah Pioneers, 1960.

Carter, Kate B., comp. *Heart Throbs of the West.* 12 vols. Salt Lake City: Daughters of Utah Pioneers, 1936-1951.

Carter, Kate B., comp. *Our Pioneer Heritage.* 20 vols. Salt Lake City: Daughters of Utah Pioneers, 1958-1977.

Carter, Kate B., comp. *Treasures of Pioneer History.* 6 vols. Salt Lake City: Daughters of Utah Pioneers, 1952-1961.

Dellenbaugh, Frederick Samuel. *A Canyon Voyage.* New York: G. P. Putham's Sons, 1908.

History of Tooele County. Salt Lake City: Daughters of Utah Pioneers, Tooele County Company, 1961.

Monuments to Courage. Beaver County Daughters of Utah Pioneers, 1948.

Perkins, Cornelia Adams, with Marian Gardner Nielson and Lenora Butt Jones, eds. *Saga of San Juan.* Salt Lake City: Mercury Publishing Co., 1957.

Ricks, Joel E., ed. *The History of a Valley.* Salt Lake City: Deseret News Publishing Co., 1956.

Roberts, B. H., ed. *A Comprehensive History of the Church of Jesus Christ of Latter-day Saints, Century One.* 6 vols. Salt Lake City: The Church of Jesus Christ of Latter-day Saints, 1930.

Roper, Margaret W. *Echoes of the Sage and Cedars.* Salt Lake City: Publisher's Press, 1970.

Reference and Bibliographical Guides

Bitton, Davis. *Guide to Mormon Diaries and Autobiographies.* Provo, Utah. Brigham Young University Press, 1977.

Flake, Chad J. *A Mormon Bibliography: 1830-1930.* Salt Lake City: University of Utah Press, 1978.

Jenson, Andrew. *Latter-day Saint Biographical Encyclopedia.* 4 vols. Salt Lake City: Andrew Jenson History Co., 1901.

Index